SHELVING
KNOW-HOW

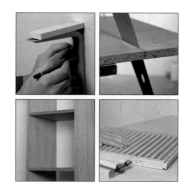

SHELVING
KNOW-HOW

Mike Lawrence

HERMES
HOUSE

This edition is published by Hermes House

Hermes House is an imprint of
Anness Publishing Ltd
Hermes House, 88–89 Blackfriars Road,
London SE1 8HA
tel. 020 7401 2077; fax 020 7633 9499;
info@anness.com

A CIP catalogue record for this book is
available from the British Library.

Publisher: Joanna Lorenz
Managing Editor: Judith Simons
Art Manager: Clare Reynolds
Project Editor: Felicity Forster
Editor: Ian Penberthy
Photographers: Colin Bowling & John Freeman
Designer: Bill Mason
Editorial Reader: Jonathan Marshall
Production Controller: Joanna King

Additional text: Mike Collins & Stephen Corbett

Previously published as *Do it Yourself Shelves
and Storage*

10 9 8 7 6 5 4 3 2 1

NOTES
The author and publishers have made
every effort to ensure that all instructions
contained within this book are accurate and
safe, and cannot accept liability for any
resulting injury, damage or loss to persons
or property, however it may arise. If in any
doubt as to the correct procedure to follow
for any home improvements task, seek
professional advice.

CONTENTS

INTRODUCTION

Finding suitable storage space around the home for all the personal and household belongings every family accumulates can be quite a challenge. One difficulty is making a sensible compromise between tidiness and accessibility; it is no good having a place for everything if that means spending hours each day laboriously taking things out and putting them back again.

The solution is to tailor-make storage to suit its purpose. Some things need a temporary resting place where they remain readily accessible. Others need long-term storage, perhaps being retrieved and used only occasionally. And there is a third storage category, that of display – simply to show things off.

In a typical home, possessions are stored in one of three main ways: on shelves, in cupboards (closets) or in drawers. These may be combined in a variety of storage or display units, and the amount of each type of space that is required will vary from one house to another. For example, the avid bookworm will have miles of bookshelves, while the clothes horse will need more wardrobe space.

The storage that is needed can be provided in one of two ways. One is to buy or make pieces of freestanding furniture that match the required storage function. The other is to use raw materials such as wood and manufactured boards plus the

BELOW: Planned storage is essential in a kitchen to make the most of available space.

ABOVE: A system of shelves provides a useful means of storage in a living room.

ABOVE: For an office/study area, consider using wire baskets for storage.

appropriate hardware to create built-in storage space – arrays of shelving, cupboards in alcoves and so on. The former is the best solution for those who value furniture more than function, since the pieces can be moved from one home to another. However, built-in storage is generally more effective in providing the most space for the least money, since the walls of a room can often be used as part of the structure. In this book, you will find a wide variety of storage options that you can use to good effect.

Apart from obvious places such as kitchen cabinets and bedroom wardrobes, there are many places in the main rooms of the home where items can be stored. This can be done without spoiling the look of the room. Properly planned storage space can be not only practical and capacious, but positively elegant.

LIVING ROOM

Here, storage needs are likely to be firmly leisure-oriented. There has to be room for books, tapes, CDs, videotapes and DVDs, not to mention display space for ornaments and other treasures. The choice is between freestanding and built-in furniture, and it is worth spending time looking at different possibilities because here looks are as important as performance.

Built-in furniture can make optimum use of alcoves and other recesses. A more radical option is a complete wall of storage units, which could incorporate space for home entertainment equipment, as well as features such as a drinks cabinet. This also offers the opportunity to include a home office section – some desk space, room for a computer, plus somewhere to file away all the essential paperwork that every household generates.

KITCHEN

Storage is a serious business here, and what is needed and how it is provided depends on what kind of kitchen it is and how it is used. The fully fitted kitchen is still popular because it packs the most storage into the least space, although there is now a discernible movement back to farmhouse-style kitchens fitted with freestanding rather than built-in furniture. This is suitable only for people who are either very tidy and well organized or, on the other hand, happy to live in chaos. The style of such kitchens restricts the amount of storage space they can offer at the expense of the look of the room, so for those who have a lot of kitchen utensils and like to keep large stocks

ABOVE: A fitted kitchen unit provides made-to-measure storage space under a work counter.

of food, a fitted kitchen is a better idea. However, there is one big advantage with freestanding furniture: it can be taken along when moving house.

In deciding what is wanted, analyze storage needs thoroughly. Think about food, utensils and small appliances for a start; all need a place close to cooking and food preparation areas. Move on to items like china, cutlery and glassware; do they need to be in the kitchen at all, or would the dining room be a better place to keep them? Then consider non-culinary items – things like cleaning materials, table linen and so on – and make sure there is enough space for them.

Remember that ceiling-height cupboards (closets) are always a better bet than ones that finish just above head height, even if some small steps

ABOVE: The traditional dresser is ideal for creating the country kitchen look.

or a box are needed to reach them. It is best to use the top shelves for storing seldom-used items.

Always aim to make the best possible use of cupboard space. Fit extra shelves where necessary, use wire baskets for ventilated storage, hang small racks on the backs of cupboard doors and use swing-out carousels to gain access to corner cupboards.

If there is a separate laundry room, it is often easier to split cooking and non-cooking storage needs by moving all home laundry and cleaning equipment out of the kitchen altogether. Such a room can also act as a useful back porch if it has access to a garden.

DINING ROOM

Here, storage needs relate mainly to providing places for china, glassware and cutlery – especially any that is kept for special occasions. Think too about storage for tablemats, cloths and other table accessories. There may also be a need for somewhere to store small appliances such as toasters, coffee makers and hotplates. Once again, the choice is between built-in storage units and freestanding furniture; this is largely a matter of taste.

HALLWAY

Simple hooks and an umbrella stand are the bare minimum, but consider providing an enclosed cupboard (closet) that is built-in rather than freestanding. It is simple to borrow

ABOVE: A collection of glasses can be seen to best advantage in a glass-fronted display case.

some porch or hall floor space to create an enclosure. If it is fitted with a door to match others leading to the rest of the house, it will blend in perfectly. Make sure it is ventilated so that damp clothes can dry.

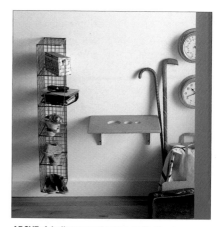

ABOVE: A hallway needs storage for items you will use outdoors, such as umbrellas and shoes.

BEDROOM

Now take a look at your storage requirements in the bedroom. Here, the main need is for space to store clothes, and this is one area where built-in (and ideally, walk-in) storage is the perfect solution. If there are two bedrooms, space can often be poached by forming a deep partition wall, accessible from one or both rooms. This can actually save money in the long run, as there is no furniture to buy. If you have bedrooms upstairs and

ABOVE: Wardrobes need an arrangement of hanging rails, shelves and drawers.

the overall upstairs floor space is large enough, you could also consider creating a separate dressing room.

Bedrooms built under the roof slope offer an opportunity to make use of the space behind the walls by creating fully lined eaves cupboards (closets). These are particularly useful for long-term storage of items such as luggage, which may be needed only occasionally, as well as providing a home for toys and games in children's rooms.

Do not just restrict bedroom storage to clothes and bedlinen, though. There is no reason why it should not also allow for books, ornaments, or even a small television or computer.

LEFT: In a bedroom, small shelves can provide useful room for a variety of bits and pieces.

RIGHT: In a home workshop, use perforated wall boards to store hand tools.

BATHROOM

Next, look at the bathroom. Here requirements are likely to be relatively low-key – somewhere to keep toiletries and cleaning materials, for example. It is not a good idea to store towels and the like in a potentially damp and steamy atmosphere. The choice is likely to be between a floor-standing vanity unit and some wall cabinets, although if space permits some thought might be given to the growing number of fully fitted bathroom furniture ranges.

ROOF SPACE

It is worth boarding over at least the area around the access hatch so that luggage, boxes and the like can be put there. If the roof construction permits, however, there is a chance to create almost unlimited storage capacity. Fit a proper ladder for safe and easy access.

WORKSHOP

An area where some storage space is certainly needed is a home workshop, whether this is a spare room, an area at the back of the garage or a separate building. The basic need is for shelf space, to take everything from cans of paint to garden products, and also some form of tool storage to keep everything in order.

LEFT: A corner cabinet makes a versatile bathroom storage unit because it uses literally every corner of space. In this bathroom, bottles and soaps have been neatly stored in an aluminium accessory holder.

RIGHT: Storage can be stylish and attractive as well as functional, as these painted bathroom hooks show.

MATERIALS & EQUIPMENT

When it comes to creating storage space around the home, you have two choices: either to buy ready-made storage units or to make your own from raw materials such as wood or boards, using proprietary hardware – support brackets or systems, hinges, connectors and so on. The following pages will give you a good idea of the materials to use for a variety of storage projects, together with the necessary tools and hardware. Carrying out any kind of do-it-yourself work requires care, since you will often be working with sharp tools and possibly hazardous substances. Always give plenty of thought to your own safety and that of others around you.

WOOD AND MANUFACTURED BOARDS

Shelves can be made of natural wood or manufactured boards. Ready-made shelves can be bought from do-it-yourself stores; they are usually made of veneered or plastic-coated chipboard (particle board). The latter traditionally have either a white or imitation woodgrain finish, but subtle pastel shades and bold primary colours are becoming more widely available. Otherwise, shelves can be cut from full-sized boards: chipboard, plywood, MDF (medium-density fiberboard) and blockboard are all suitable.

ABOVE: Pine is a softwood that is readily available and easily worked. It can have an attractive grain pattern.

BOARDS

The two boards most often used are plywood and chipboard. The former, which has good mechanical strength and can be sawn easily, is suitable for structural work. Chipboard is more friable and less easy to work accurately, but is cheap. It is adequate for kitchen cabinets and bookcases. It is unwise to drive screws or nails into the edge of a chipboard panel, as the material will crumble.

Both plywood and chipboard are available faced with hardwood and coloured melamine veneer for improved appearance.

Blockboard, which consists of solid wooden blocks sandwiched between plywood skins, is a stable and strong structural material often used where some form of weight-bearing capacity is required. As with all manufactured boards, the extremely hard resins used to bond blockboard together rapidly blunt tools unless they are tungsten (carbide) tipped.

Pineboard is like the core of blockboard, but without the outer layers. Small strips of pine are glued together on edge and sanded smooth. It is ideal for shelving and carcassing.

MDF is another useful material. Unlike most other boards, it can be worked to fine detail with saws and chisels.

STANDARD SIZES

Nearly all manufactured boards have a standard size of 1220 x 2440mm (4 x 8ft). Some suppliers offer a metric size, which is smaller (1200 x 2400mm), so always check, as this can make a

ABOVE: Sawing veneered chipboard (particle board) is best done with the veneer face-up to avoid damage.

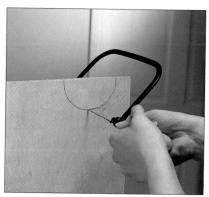

ABOVE: Plywood is easy to cut and very good for carcassing work, since it has good structural strength. A variety of thicknesses is available.

critical difference to your cutting list. Special sizes of plywood and MDF, up to 3m (10ft) in length, are available from some suppliers. Many stores will offer part sheets or cut large sheets into smaller sizes if requested at the time of purchase.

GRAIN DIRECTION

The direction in which the grain runs on the outer layers is always given first when describing plywood. This can be important when planning your cutting list. With birch plywood, for example, 1220 x 2440mm (4 x 8ft) in a supplier's catalogue will indicate that the grain runs across the width of the board, not down its length.

Most veneered decorative boards are produced with the grain running along the length, so their catalogue entries would read 2440 x 1220mm (8 x 4ft).

COMMON THICKNESSES OF MANUFACTURED BOARD

TYPE	3mm ⅛in	6mm ¼in	9mm ⅜in	12mm ½in	16mm ⅝in	19mm ¾in	22mm ⅞in	25mm 1in	32mm 1¼in
Plywood	✓	✓	✓	✓	✓	✓	✓	✓	
Plywood (Douglas fir)			✓		✓				
Blockboard						✓		✓	
Chipboard				✓	✓	✓	✓	✓	
Hardboard	✓	✓							
MDF		✓	✓	✓		✓		✓	✓

TOOLS

Measuring and marking out are common tasks. A retractable steel measuring tape will take care of the former, while a combination square will allow you to mark cutting lines at 90 and 45 degrees. For other angles, an adjustable bevel gauge will be required. A craft knife can be used for marking the cutting lines.

A spirit (carpenter's) level is essential for finding a true horizontal or vertical.

For driving nails, a claw hammer is the ideal general-purpose tool, but for small pins (brads), the narrow end of a cross-pein hammer is better. You will need a nail punch to punch nail heads below the surface of the work.

Various sizes of screwdriver for slotted, Phillips and Pozidriv screws will be necessary.

G-clamps are useful for holding items together temporarily.

Saws are also essential. Choose a general-purpose hand saw for large sections of wood and a tenon saw for smaller work. A powered circular saw will be invaluable for cutting large panels and will ensure straight cuts, while a jigsaw (saber saw) will allow curved cuts to be made in boards and thin wood. For drilling holes, a cordless drill will be most convenient.

A powered router will make short work of cutting rebates (rabbets) and slots in boards and wood. Use a jack plane for shaping wood, and bevel-edged chisels to make cutouts and recesses. Abrasive paper is essential for giving a final finish to wood.

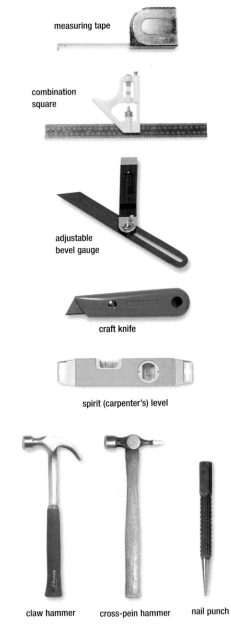

measuring tape

combination square

adjustable bevel gauge

craft knife

spirit (carpenter's) level

claw hammer   cross-pein hammer   nail punch

G-clamp

hand saw

screwdrivers

tenon saw

circular
saw

jigsaw
(saber saw)

cordless drill

jack
plane

router

bevel-edged chisel

abrasive
papers

NAILS, SCREWS AND DRILL BITS

There is no such thing as an "ordinary" nail. All nails have been designed for specific purposes, although some of them can be put to several uses.

Wire, lost-head and oval nails can be used for general carpentry. Oval nails can be driven below the surface of the work with less likelihood of them splitting the wood.

Cut nails have a tapering, rectangular section, which gives them excellent holding properties.

Panel pins (brads) are used for fixing thin panels and cladding. They are nearly always punched below the surface, as are veneer pins.

When there is a need to secure thin or fragile sheet material, such as plasterboard (gypsum board), large-headed nails are used. These are commonly called clout nails, but may also be found under specific names, such as plasterboard nails.

The holding power of screws is much greater than that of nails, and items that have been screwed together can easily be taken apart again without damage to the components.

There are various types of screw head, the most common being the slotted screw head, followed by the Phillips head and the Pozidriv head, both of which have a cruciform pattern to take the screwdriver blade.

Drill bits come in a bewildering array of sizes and types but only a few are needed by the do-it-yourselfer, such as dowel bits for flat-bottomed holes, flat bits, which cut large holes very rapidly, and twist bits, which make small holes and are used for starting screws.

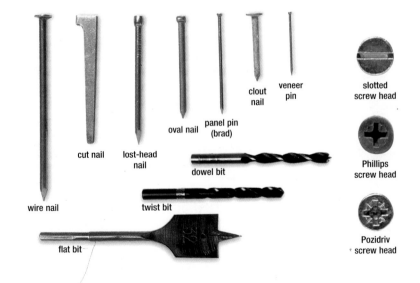

cut nail

lost-head nail

oval nail

panel pin (brad)

clout nail

veneer pin

wire nail

dowel bit

twist bit

flat bit

slotted screw head

Phillips screw head

Pozidriv screw head

FIXTURES

Wall-mounted shelving is one of two basic types – fixed or adjustable. With fixed shelving, each shelf is supported independently of others using two or more shelf brackets, which are fixed to the wall and to the underside of the shelf itself. With adjustable shelving, the shelves are carried on brackets, studs or tongues, which are slotted or clipped into vertical strips screwed to the wall.

Fixed brackets are ideal for putting up a single shelf – over a radiator, for example – although they can equally well be used to support several shelves. They come in many styles, shapes and colours. Metal brackets are the most usual, but wooden ones in various finishes are also available.

SHELF SUPPORTS

Simple metal brackets are readily available. They are fixed to the wall with screws and wall plugs, and then a wooden shelf is secured from below with screws. Shaped wooden brackets give a traditional look and are plugged to the wall in a similar way. Glass shelving for the bathroom may be fixed with shelf-grips, which are backed with adhesive strips for securing to ceramic tiles. Shelves over radiators are often of coated steel with a woodgrain decorative finish. They simply clip into place over the radiators.

Heavy-duty wall brackets are required to hold the weight of a television. These are made of metal and allow the television to be rotated through 360 degrees and tilted downward.

Small shelves can be supported in a variety of ways, including using screw eyes, dowels and lengths of wood. All these methods are suitable for shelving that will carry little weight.

Shelving systems are available from many sources. Often, they offer great flexibility and lots of add-on accessories. Many can be used as room dividers and as portable furniture.

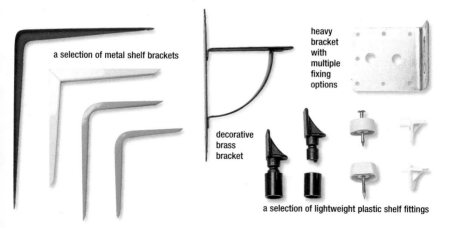

a selection of metal shelf brackets

heavy bracket with multiple fixing options

decorative brass bracket

a selection of lightweight plastic shelf fittings

HEALTH AND SAFETY

Your personal safety should underlie every stage of woodworking practice, including the layout of a workshop. It is better to plan your work to eliminate hazards rather than accommodate them – for example, wearing a dust mask and using a dust extractor on a machine that creates a lot of dust is a better solution than wearing a dust mask alone.

Because working with wood depends on the use of sharp cutting tools, cutting yourself may seem a risk that cannot be avoided, but any professional will tell you that a sharp tool is actually less dangerous than a blunt one or a tool that is used incorrectly.

fire extinguisher

PERSONAL SAFETY

• Avoid wearing loose clothing and jewellery when working, especially with machinery and power tools.

• Stout boots should be worn – a sheet of plywood will be painful if it slips and lands on your toe.

• For a better grip, wear leather gloves when handling wood and boards.

• Always inspect wood for splinters and protruding nails before picking it up.

• Always have a first aid kit in the workshop for minor injuries.

• When you work on large machines, do not work alone in case of injury.

SAFETY EQUIPMENT

Even though a private workshop is not required to comply with the health and safety legislation that applies to commercial premises, it makes sense to observe the same safety disciplines and use the personal protection equipment that is recommended and readily available. One particular danger to be aware of is fire. Wood is flammable and so are some of the materials used when working with wood. It is advisable not to smoke when working with flammable materials, and always have a fire extinguisher to hand.

FIRST AID KIT

Obtain the correct size of kit recommended for small workshops, and keep it in a prominent position ready for use. If any of the contents are used, replace them immediately.

EYE PROTECTION

Always protect your eyes with safety glasses or goggles when sanding, finishing or using power tools. When operating a machine that produces large quantities of chippings at high speed, wear a full-face visor.

EAR PROTECTION

When using power tools or machinery, wear approved ear protectors or earplugs to keep noise to an acceptable level. Some people think that it is safer to operate a machine by listening to its performance. They are wrong, and they risk permanent impairment of their hearing in the future.

DUST EXTRACTION

By far the best way of reducing the risk of inhaling sawdust is to install a dust extraction system. Compact units designed for the small workshop are available from all good tool suppliers. Many portable power tools have self-contained dust extraction systems or are supplied with adaptors for direct connection to an extraction unit.

DUST MASKS

There are several types of mask to choose from, including the frame mask with replaceable pads and disposable masks that cover the whole of the mouth and nose. Choose the right product for the level of dust generated in the workshop. The dust produced by sanding machines is the most hazardous and needs a mask with a fine filter. Use

sanders that are fitted with their own dust collection bags to cut down on the amount of dust produced. Clear, full-face safety masks are available and are easy to put on and comfortable to wear.

When working with hazardous finishing materials, keep the workshop well ventilated and wear a respirator if necessary. Always be guided by the manufacturer's safety data. In general, if a product is so dangerous as to cause potentially serious problems, you should consider an alternative.

GLOVES AND BOOTS

It is advisable to wear heavy-duty rigger's gloves to protect your hands when using sawn wood or large, heavy sheets of material. When you are using adhesives or finishing materials that are harmful to the skin, wear rubber or latex gloves. It is best to wear sensible and sturdy boots to keep toes protected in case you drop any wood or a sharp or heavy tool.

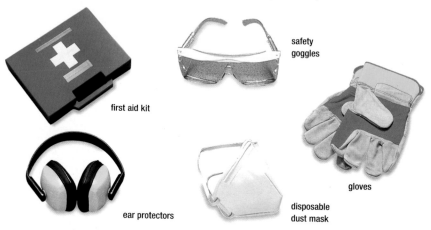

safety goggles

first aid kit

ear protectors

disposable dust mask

gloves

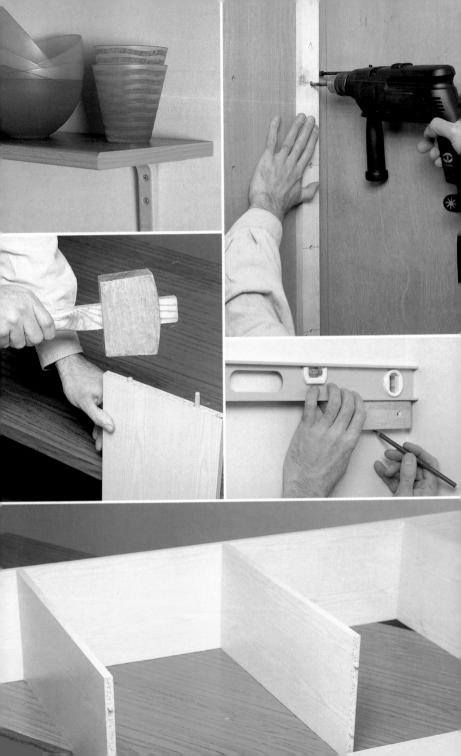

SHELVES

The most basic form of storage is shelving, but even so, there are options to consider. Adjustable shelving systems are very versatile, making use of slotted wall uprights that accept special shelf brackets. They allow you to add or remove shelves or adjust their spacing at will. Individual brackets are ideal for single shelves, but can be utilitarian in appearance. If you intend fitting shelves into an alcove, they can be fixed to battens screwed to the wall. In a freestanding unit, shelves can be held by special studs, bookcase strips or dowel-reinforced butt joints. In a garage or home workshop, shelves can be supported on sturdy "ladder" frames to create flexible storage systems.

ADJUSTABLE SHELVING

Shelving systems abound in do-it-yourself stores for those who prefer simply to fit rather than to make the shelving. There is a range of brackets on the market to cater for every need, and these clip into slotted uprights screwed to the wall. The bracket positions can be adjusted to vary the spacing between the shelves to accommodate your needs.

Shelving systems are a versatile way of dealing with changing requirements, and they have the distinct advantage of being portable when you need to move them. They are capable of holding heavy weights, but remember that ultimately a shelf's capacity depends on the strength of the wall fixing employed.

First measure the distance between the shelving uprights, bearing in mind the thickness and material to be used for the shelf. Books can be very heavy, so do not set the uprights too far apart, otherwise the shelf will sag in the middle. About a quarter of the length of the shelf can overhang each end. If necessary, cut the uprights to length. Drill and plug the wall so that you can attach one upright by its topmost hole. Do not tighten the screw fully at this stage. Simply allow the upright to hang freely.

Hold your spirit (carpenter's) level against the side of the upright, and when you are satisfied that it is vertical, mark its position lightly on the wall with a pencil. Mark in the remaining screw positions, then drill and plug the rest of the screw holes.

You may find that when you tighten the screws, the upright needs a little packing here and there to keep it vertical in the other plane. If these discrepancies are not too large, this adjustment can be done by varying the relative tightness of the screws, which will pull the upright into line. You can mark off the position for the second upright and any others, using a spirit level on top of a shelf with a couple of brackets slipped into position. Fitting the second upright entails the same procedure as before.

PLANNING SHELVES

Aim to keep everyday items within easy reach and position deep shelves near the bottom so that it is easy to see and reach the back. Allow 25–50mm (1–2in) of clearance on top of the height of objects, so that they are easy to take down.

Think about weight too. If the shelves will store heavy objects, the shelving material must be chosen with care. With 12mm (½in) chipboard (particle board) and readymade veneered or melamine-faced shelves, space brackets at 450mm (18in) for heavy loads or 600mm (2ft) for light loads. With 19mm (¾in) chipboard or 12mm (½in) plywood, increase the spacing to 600mm (2ft) and 750mm (2ft 6in) respectively. For 19mm (¾in) plywood, blockboard, MDF (medium-density fiberboard) or natural wood, the bracket spacing can be 750mm (2ft 6in) for heavy loads, 900mm (3ft) for light ones.

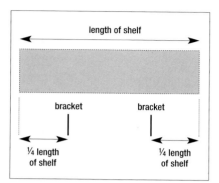

1 Measure the distance between the uprights. Allow a quarter length of shelf at each end.

2 Fix the first screw loosely in the top hole and let the upright hang.

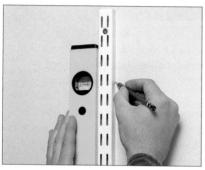

3 Check the bracket is absolutely vertical with a spirit (carpenter's) level.

4 A little packing card may be necessary if the wall is uneven.

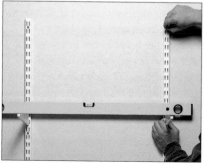

5 Mark the position for the second upright using the first as a guide.

6 The shelf brackets can be inserted at different heights and can be easily moved.

USING SHELF BRACKETS

With a little thought, shelving can be made to be decorative as well as functional, and a variety of materials, including wood, metal and glass, can be used to good effect.

All require firm wall fixings. Always use a spirit (carpenter's) level when fitting shelves.

SIMPLE SHELVING

Ready-made shelving systems can be employed, both wall-mounted and freestanding. The basic methods of fitting shelving are the same, no matter what material is used. Essential requirements are establishing a truly level surface with a spirit level, obtaining firm fixings in the wall, and being able to fit the shelving accurately into an alcove.

The simplest form of shelf is a wooden board supported by a pair of metal or wooden brackets. The latter are available in a range of sizes and in styles that vary from purely functional to quite decorative. Consider carefully before buying; the brackets will be in plain view, so make sure they fit in with their surroundings. You can make them less obvious, however, by painting them to match the wall colour.

Make sure that you match the size of bracket to the width of board you intend using – if too narrow, the shelf will not be

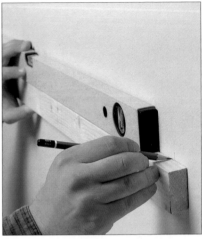

1 Mark the position of the shelf by drawing a line across the wall, using a long, straight batten as a guide. Make sure it is perfectly horizontal with a spirit (carpenter's) level.

supported fully and may actually collapse when loaded. Choose brackets that will span between two-thirds and three-quarters of the width of the board.

Use your spirit level to ascertain the height and horizontal run of the shelf, then mark the positions for the brackets. Mark the positions of the screws through the holes in the brackets, drill with a masonry bit and insert wall plugs. Hold each bracket in place and start all the screws into the wall plugs before tightening them fully.

If fitting more than one shelf on an uninterrupted run of wall, mark them out at the same time, using a try or combination square. Cut them to size, then screw them to the shelf brackets.

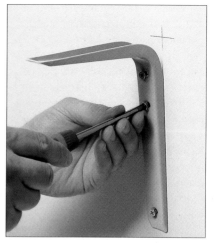

2 Mark the positions of the fixing screws on the wall through the bracket holes. For accuracy, lay a short piece of wood on top of each bracket, aligning it with the pencil line.

3 Drill the holes for the screws, using a masonry bit if necessary, and insert wall plugs. Hold each bracket in place and start all of its screws before tightening them fully.

4 Lay the shelf on top of the brackets, making sure the overhang is equal at each end. Use a bradawl (awl) to make pilot holes and screw through the brackets into the shelf.

5 You can also attach the shelf to the brackets before mounting the brackets to the wall. If you do this, make sure that the back edge of the shelf aligns with the bracket mounting faces.

FITTING SHELVES IN ALCOVES

Alcoves beside chimney breasts (fireplace projections) or other obstructions make perfect sites for shelves, since the back and side walls can be used as supports. Although it is easy to use fixed shelf brackets or an adjustable shelving system to support shelves here, it is cheaper to fix slim wood or metal support strips directly to the alcove walls and rest the shelves on top of these.

If using wooden supports, cut their front ends at an angle so that they are less noticeable when the shelves are fitted. Paint them the same colour as the walls (or to tone with the wall covering) to make them even less obtrusive. If using L-shaped metal strips for the supports, choose a size that matches the shelf thickness so they are almost invisible once the shelves have been fitted.

The actual job is quite simple. Mark the shelf level on the alcove walls, cut the supports to the required lengths and screw them to the walls. Then cut your shelf to size and slip it into place, resting on the supports. It can be nailed, screwed or glued in place for extra stability. The only difficult part is in making the shelf a good fit, since the alcove walls may not be truly square. Accurate measuring of the alcove width at front and back, plus some careful scribing of the rear edge of the shelf, will ensure good results.

When fitting more than one shelf, measure for each separately, since the alcove may not be uniform in size.

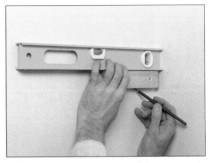

1 Decide on the shelf positions, then use a spirit (carpenter's) level to mark the position of the first shelf support on one alcove wall.

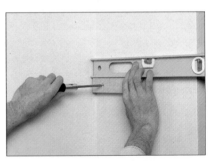

4 Screw the second support in place as before, marking the positions of the fixing holes on the wall. Check again that it is level.

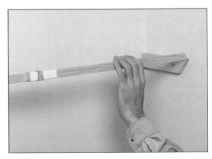

7 Repeat step 5 to measure the width at the point where the front edge of the shelf will be, then transfer the measurement to the shelf.

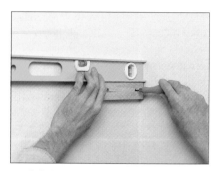

2 Drill clearance holes in the supports, and use one to mark its fixing hole positions on the wall. Drill the holes and fix this support.

3 Rest a shelf on the first support, hold it level and mark the shelf position on the opposite wall. Then prepare the second shelf support.

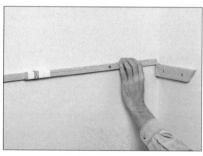

5 Make a set of gauge rods from scrap wood, held together with a rubber band. Extend the rods to span the rear wall of the alcove.

6 Lift the rods out carefully without disturbing their positions and lay them on the rear edge of the shelf. Mark the width of the alcove on it.

8 Cut the shelf to width and lay it in place. If the fit is poor against the back wall, use a block and pencil to scribe the wall outline on it.

9 Saw carefully along the scribed line with a power jigsaw (saber saw). Sand the cut edge smooth and fit the shelf back in position.

USING SHELF SUPPORT STRIPS

This is an ingenious method of providing support for single shelves. It consists of a specially shaped channel that is screwed to the wall at the required position; then the shelf is simply knocked into place with a soft-faced mallet.

The channel grips the shelf securely and can support surprisingly heavy loads. For lighter loads such as ornaments you can use small shelf support blocks. The shelf is clamped in place by tightening a locking screw underneath the block.

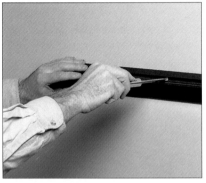

1 Hold the support strip against the wall at the desired level and mark the position of the central screw hole. Drill and plug the hole, then attach the strip.

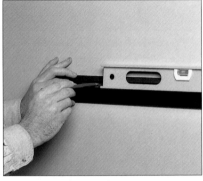

2 Place a spirit (carpenter's) level on top of the strip. Swivel the strip until it is precisely level, then mark the positions of the remaining screw holes on the wall.

3 Swivel the strip out of the way and drill the other holes. Insert wall plugs. Then secure the strip with the remaining screws and slot the shelf into place.

4 Shelf support blocks are also available for mounting small display shelves. The shelf is clamped in the block by tightening a locking screw from underneath.

USING STUDS AND BOOKCASE STRIPS

Adjustable shelves may also be wanted inside a storage unit. There are two options. The first involves drilling a series of carefully aligned holes in each side of the unit, then inserting small plastic or metal shelf support studs. The second uses what is known as bookcase strip – a metal moulding with slots into which small pegs or tongues are fitted to support the shelves. Two strips are needed at each side of the unit. In both cases, accurate marking out is essential to ensure that the supports line up.

USING SHELF SUPPORT STUDS

1 Use a simple predrilled jig to make the holes for the shelf supports in the sides of the unit. A depth stop will prevent you from drilling too deep and breaking through.

2 Drill two sets of holes in each side of the unit, with the top of the jig held against the top of the unit to guarantee alignment. Insert the supports and fit the shelves.

USING BOOKCASE STRIPS

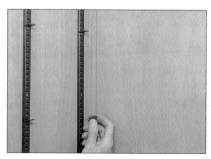

1 Mark the positions of the top ends of the strips to ensure that they are level, then mark the screw positions to a true vertical. Make pilot holes and screw on the strips.

2 Insert pairs of pegs into the bookcase strip at each shelf position, checking that their lugs are properly engaged in the slots. Then lift the shelf into place on the pegs.

FREESTANDING SHELVING

Freestanding shelf units can easily be moved if the room layout is changed or when painting or papering. However, they have drawbacks too. Some manufactured shelving and display units are rather flimsy, and may twist out of square or sag if they are heavily loaded. In general, better results come from building units from stronger materials such as natural wood and plywood.

The other problem is getting units to stand upright against the wall; skirtings (baseboards) prevent standard units from being pushed back flush with the wall surface, and carpet gripper strips make them lean forwards slightly. The answer is to design the side supports on the cantilever principle with just one point of contact with the floor. This point should be as far as possible from the wall, so that the unit presses more firmly against the wall as the load on the shelves is increased. Fix the unit to the wall with brackets for safety, particularly if there are children around.

Since a shelf unit is basically a box with internal dividers, it can be constructed in several different ways, using simple butt joints or more complicated housings. Perhaps the best compromise between strength and ease of construction is to use glued butt joints reinforced with hardwood dowels, which give the joints the extra rigidity they need in a unit of this sort.

Start by deciding on the dimensions of the unit, then select materials to suit the loading the shelves will support.

1 Clamp groups of identical parts together. Mark them to length and cut them in one go to ensure that they are all the same.

4 Glue the dowels and tap them into the holes in the shelf ends. Check that they all project by the same amount, and cut down any that may be too long.

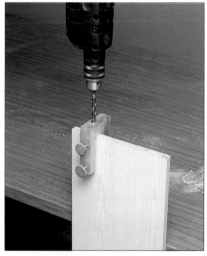

2 Mark the positions of the shelf dowel holes on the unit sides. Drill them all to the required depth, using a drill stand if possible.

3 Use a dowelling jig to drill the dowel holes in the shelf ends. This ensures that the holes are correctly positioned and are drilled straight.

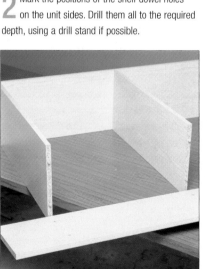

5 Assemble the unit by gluing one end of each of the three shelves and joining them to one of the side panels. Then glue the other ends and add the second side panel.

6 Cut a hardboard or plywood backing panel. Use a try square to check that the angles are correct, then pin the board into position on the back of the unit.

MAKING UTILITY SHELVING

Storage space in workshops, garages, basements and attics is best provided by building simple but sturdy shelves from inexpensive materials. Use wood that is sawn, not planed (dressed), for the framework, and cut the shelves from scrap plywood. Damaged boards and offcuts (scraps) are often available cheaply from timber merchants (lumberyards).

The shelving units shown here are made from 50mm (2in) square wood, with shelves of 19mm (¾in) plywood.

The only other materials needed are some scraps of 9mm (⅜in) thick plywood for the small triangular braces that help to stiffen the structure.

The uprights should be spaced about 760mm (2ft 6in) apart so that the shelves will not sag; they can reach right to ceiling level if desired. Match the depth of the unit to whatever is to be stored and to the amount of space available. Remember that it can be difficult reaching things at the back of deep shelves.

1 Start by deciding on the height the uprights should be, and on how many "ladders" are needed. Cut them all to length with a power saw.

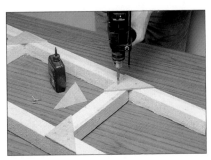

2 Make up the ladders by gluing and nailing the rungs between pairs of uprights. Reinforce the joints by gluing and screwing on plywood triangles.

3 Stand the assembled ladders against the wall, check that they are truly vertical, and screw them to the wall into wooden studs or masonry anchors.

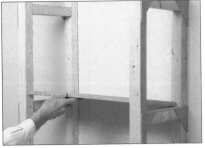

4 Cut as many plywood shelves as are needed so they span between the centre lines of the rungs; notch the corners so they will fit neatly.

MAKING A STORAGE RACK

This tool storage rack is basically a wall-mounted backing board of 19mm (¾in) thick plywood. Tools are hung on various supports, as shown in the illustration. These are located in, and slide along, horizontal channels formed by pinning 38 x 12mm (1½ x ½in) plywood to the backing panel and then pinning 75 x 19mm (3 x ¾in) softwood strips to the plywood. Make the trays for small tools from 12mm (½in) plywood, and use hardwood dowel pegs or old wire coat hangers to form support hooks for larger tools. Slide the back plate of each support into its channel at the sides of the rack, and push them to where they are needed.

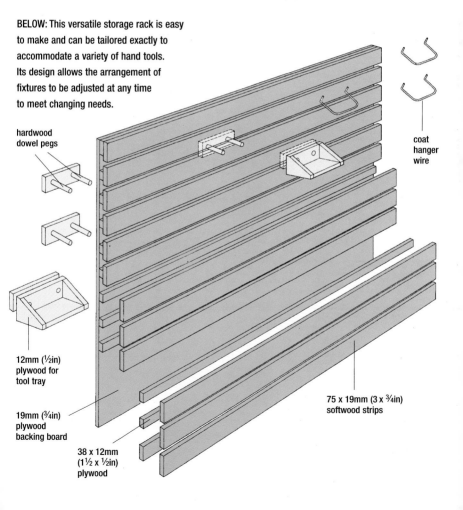

BELOW: This versatile storage rack is easy to make and can be tailored exactly to accommodate a variety of hand tools. Its design allows the arrangement of fixtures to be adjusted at any time to meet changing needs.

hardwood dowel pegs

coat hanger wire

12mm (½in) plywood for tool tray

19mm (¾in) plywood backing board

38 x 12mm (1½ x ½in) plywood

75 x 19mm (3 x ¾in) softwood strips

MAKING A GARAGE STORAGE WALL

The garage is a favourite place to store all manner of things, including tools and materials for do-it-yourself, gardening and car maintenance tasks. Unless these are kept under control, they will spill over until there is no room for the car. The solution is to build a shallow full-height storage unit along either the side or the end wall of the garage, tailor-made to suit whatever will be stored there.

The design concept of the storage wall is quite simple. The structure is based on ladder frames fixed to the wall to support shelves, drawers and

BELOW: This simple storage wall unit is the ideal home for all the various tools, equipment and do-it-yourself materials that are likely to find a home in your garage, keeping the floor area clear for your car. You can easily adapt its design to fit your own garage and particular needs.

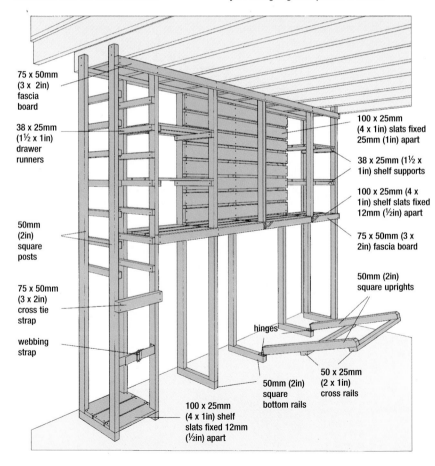

75 x 50mm (3 x 2in) fascia board

38 x 25mm (1½ x 1in) drawer runners

50mm (2in) square posts

75 x 50mm (3 x 2in) cross tie strap

webbing strap

100 x 25mm (4 x 1in) slats fixed 25mm (1in) apart

38 x 25mm (1½ x 1in) shelf supports

100 x 25mm (4 x 1in) shelf slats fixed 12mm (½in) apart

75 x 50mm (3 x 2in) fascia board

50mm (2in) square uprights

hinges

50 x 25mm (2 x 1in) cross rails

50mm (2in) square bottom rails

100 x 25mm (4 x 1in) shelf slats fixed 12mm (½in) apart

whatever else is required. The frame is made mainly from 50mm (2in) square sawn softwood, with 75 x 25mm (3 x 1in) wood for the shelves and the slatted hanging rack. The hinged section drops down to allow sheets of plywood and the like to be placed on edge behind it, and is held shut with a simple hasp and staple at each side. The wall-mounted rack allows heavy items to be hung out of the way, yet be readily to hand, on metal S-hooks.

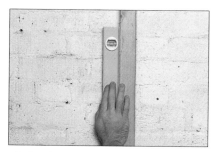

1 Start by securing the uprights to the garage wall to form the various bays. Check that each is vertical before fixing it in place.

2 Set sole plates on something damp-proof (here sheet vinyl flooring has been used), and screw them down into expanding wall plugs in holes drilled in the garage floor.

3 Simply nail the components together as required to form the frames that make up each bay. Add horizontals to support wooden shelves or plastic bowl drawers.

4 To make the drop-down flap for the sheet materials storage bay, hinge the two front uprights to their baseplates and add a cross rail.

5 To make the wall rack, nail on the slats, using an offcut (scrap) as a spacer. Make the shelves in the same way.

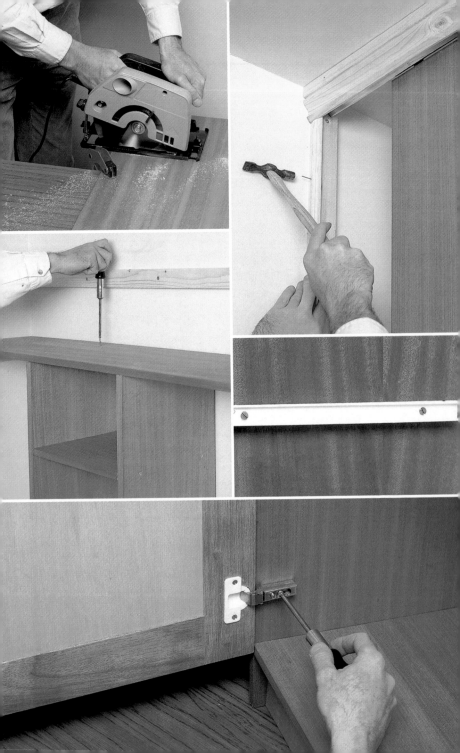

CABINETS & WARDROBES

Cabinetmaking is a skilled craft, but the ready availability of man-made boards faced with veneer or melamine and ready-made doors in a variety of styles has made it possible for any competent do-it-yourselfer to create attractive, functional cabinets for any room of the home. Panels can be joined by simple glued butt joints reinforced with nails, screws or wooden dowels, while doors can be hung with flush or concealed hinges. Even drawers can be added, using kits of plastic parts. Wardrobe space is invariably in short supply in the bedroom, but it is relatively simple to add doors, shelves and hanging rails to an alcove, or even across the entire end wall of a room.

MAKING CABINETS

Freestanding storage units consist simply of a basic box, fitted out internally as required. For example, this can include one or more shelves, vertical dividers, hanging rails, drawers and doors. All this applies to units as diverse in scale as a small hi-fi cabinet and a large double wardrobe. A pair of boxes can be placed under a counter top to create a desk or dressing table.

Units will probably be made from manufactured boards. It is difficult to get natural wood wider than about 225mm (9in), which rather restricts its scope; it is also more expensive. The most popular material for making box furniture is chipboard (particle board), especially the veneered and melamine-faced varieties. It is sold in planks and boards of various sizes with the long edges (and sometimes the ends) already veneered or faced. Its main disadvantage is that it will sag under its own weight across spans of more than about 900mm (3ft).

Stronger alternatives are plywood, MDF (medium-density fiberboard) and blockboard. Blockboard is the strongest and can be used unsupported over spans twice as great as for chipboard. Sheets of blockboard sold as door blanks usually have the long edges faced.

Plywood offers the best of both worlds – it is almost as strong as blockboard, and has edges that can be neatly finished. It is also available in thicknesses from 4mm (just over ⅛in) to 19mm (¾in), so there should be a perfect match for any application.

MDF is a popular choice for box furniture as well as shelves, since it cuts beautifully without the need for finishing sawn edges. It is a medium-strength material and its very smooth surface finish can be painted, varnished or stained. Available in 2440 x 1220mm (8 x 4ft) sheets and in thicknesses

MAKING BUTT JOINTS

1 To make a box, take measurements and start by cutting the components to size. Use a circular saw or a jigsaw (saber saw).

4 Reinforce a glued joint with nails driven in so that they pass into the centre of the panel underneath. Use a damp cloth to remove any excess adhesive.

ranging from 6 to 25mm (¼ to 1in), MDF falls into the medium price range.

Those who are inexperienced in using power tools to make rebates (rabbets) and housing joints will be making boxes using glued butt joints, nailed or screwed for extra strength. These are adequate for small items, but will need reinforcing on larger pieces. The ideal way of doing this is with hardwood dowels. It is advisable to use dowels for chipboard, in which nails and even screws will not hold well. Alternatives, for light loads only, are special chipboard screws, or ordinary screws set in glued-in fibre wall plugs.

2 Label each piece in pencil and mark both halves of each joint with matching letters to avoid mix-ups during assembly.

3 To make a glued butt joint, spread adhesive along the edge of one component. Assemble the joint and clamp it to keep it square.

5 Screwed joints are stronger than nailed ones. Place the edge component against the face component and mark its position on the latter. Mark the screw positions carefully.

6 Drill clearance holes through the face component, then pilot holes in the edge component. Countersink the clearance holes and drive in chipboard (particle board) screws.

USING DOWELS

Hardwood dowels are an effective means of reinforcing butt joints between panels, and you can buy them in various sizes. Since they are glued into blind holes, it is essential to allow glue to escape as they are pushed home. This can be achieved by sanding a "flat" along the length of the dowel or by using ready-grooved dowels.

Careful marking out and drilling is essential to ensure correct alignment of the dowel holes in adjacent panels. Various devices are available to make this possible. The simplest is the dowel pin. This is fitted into the dowel hole in one panel, which is pushed against the adjoining panel; a sharp point on the pin effectively marks the centre of the dowel hole in that panel, ensuring perfect alignment. Another method is a dowelling jig, which fits over the edges of the panels to align the holes.

1 Draw a pencil line along the centre of the joint position, then align the two components carefully and mark corresponding dowel hole positions on both pieces.

2 Drill the dowel holes in the face component, using a depth stop to avoid drilling too deep and breaking through the panel. Use a dowelling jig to drill holes in board edges.

3 Insert glued dowels in the holes in the edge component, then glue this to the face component. Add more glue along the joint line to provide extra strength.

4 A back panel will give any box extra strength, and also helps to resist skewing. Cut the panel fractionally undersize, then nail it in place, making sure the assembly is square first.

FITTING FLUSH HINGES

A dding doors and drawers to a basic storage box will turn it into a cabinet or a chest. Doors can be hung on any one of the many types of hinge available, but two of the most versatile are the flush hinge and the concealed hinge. The former has one leaf fitting into a cut-out in the other, and so can be surface-mounted to the door edge and the frame, without the need to cut recesses.

These hinges have countersunk mounting screw holes in their leaves, so it is essential to buy screws that have heads that fit the countersinks exactly. If the heads are too big, they will prevent the screws from sitting flush with the faces of the hinge leaves and will stop the doors from closing.

1 Mark the hinge position on the door edge, then make pilot holes and screw the smaller flap to the door. Check that the hinge knuckle faces the right way.

2 Hold the door in position against the cabinet carcass, and mark the hinge position on it. Mark the screw holes too, then drill pilot holes for the screws.

3 Reposition the door and attach the larger hinge leaf to the carcass. Check the door alignment carefully, then attach the other hinge in the same way.

FITTING CONCEALED HINGES

The concealed hinge is a little more complex to fit – the hinge body sits in a round hole bored in the rear face of the door, while the hinge arm is attached to a baseplate fitted to the side of the cabinet carcass – but it can be adjusted after fitting to ensure perfect alignment on multi-door installations.

Make in-out adjustments to the door by loosening the mounting screw and repositioning the door. Make side-to-side adjustments with the smaller screw.

1 Mark the centre line of the hinge baseplate on the side of the cabinet, then lay the door flat against the carcass and extend the line on to it.

2 Use a power drill fitted with an end mill, held in a drill stand, to bore the recess for the hinge body to the required depth in the rear face of the cabinet door.

3 Press the hinge body into the recess, check that the arm is at right-angles to the door edge and make pilot holes for the fixing screws. Drive these in.

4 Next, attach the baseplate to the side of the cabinet, centred on the guideline drawn earlier. Check that it is fitted correctly.

5 Hold the door against the cabinet, slot the hinge arm over the screw on the baseplate and tighten the screw to lock the hinge arm in place.

MAKING UP DRAWER KITS

When it comes to adding drawers to your cabinets, the simplest solution is to use plastic drawer kits. These consist of moulded sections that interlock to form the sides and back of the drawer, special corner blocks to allow a drawer front of any chosen material to be attached, and a base (usually a piece of enamelled hardboard). The drawer sides are grooved to fit over plastic runners that are screwed to the cabinet sides. The sides, back and base can be cut down to size if necessary.

1 Cut the sides and back to size if necessary, then stick the side and back sections together, using the clips and adhesive provided in the kit.

2 Cut the base down in size too if the drawer size was altered. Then slide the panel into place in the grooves in the side and back sections.

3 Screw the two corner joint blocks to the inner face of the drawer front, stick on the drawer base support channel, and glue the front to the ends of the side sections.

4 Hold the drawer within the cabinet to mark the positions of its side grooves on the side walls. Then attach the plastic drawer runners with the screws provided.

FITTING BUILT-IN WARDROBES

The walls of a room can be used to create larger storage spaces. These can range from filling in an alcove, through a unit in the corner of a room, to one running right across the room to the opposite wall. If the room has a central chimney breast (fireplace projection) with an alcove at each side, both alcoves can be used for storage and the chimney breast can be concealed with dummy doors.

In each case, the most important part is a frame to support the doors; these can be hinged conventionally or suspended from ceiling-mounted track. Remember that hinged doors allow unlimited access, but need floor space in front of them so they can be opened easily. Sliding doors do not need this floor space, but they do have the minor disadvantage that access to the interior is sometimes restricted – when one door is open, it blocks access to the next section.

Such a flexible structure affords an opportunity to meet storage needs precisely. Start by selecting the depth needed for clothes to hang freely on hanging rails, then work out what width should be given to hanging space and what to shelving, drawers or basket space for storing other items of clothing. Shoe racks can be added at floor level.

Doors can be made into a feature of the room, or painted or covered to blend unobtrusively with the room's colour scheme. Large flat-surfaced doors become almost invisible if decorated with a wallcovering.

1 Screw a track support strip to the ceiling joists, levelling it with packing, then add the top track. Leave a gap at the wall for the side upright.

4 Use a spirit (carpenter's) level to check that the upright is vertical, mark its position on the wall and drill the clearance and fixing holes.

7 Hang each door by engaging the hanger wheels on the track as shown and lowering the door to the vertical position. Finally, fit the floor guides provided.

2 Hold the lengths of wood that will form the side frame uprights against the wall, and mark on them the profile of the skirting (baseboard).

3 Use a coping saw or power jigsaw (saber saw) to cut away the waste wood from the foot of the upright, then test fit against the wall.

5 Realign the upright with the positioning marks made earlier and screw it to the wall. Repeat the process at the other side of the opening.

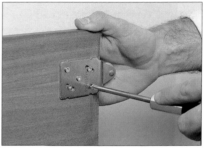

6 Cut the doors to size if necessary, allowing for clearances or overlaps as required in the door gear instructions, then fit the door hangers.

8 Conceal the track and door hangers by pinning (tacking) a decorative moulding to the track support batten. Some tracks come complete with a metal pelmet strip.

9 Finish off the installation by pinning slim wooden mouldings to the front edges of the side uprights. These hide any slight gaps when the doors are closed.

FITTING CLOTHES ORGANIZERS

In both freestanding and built-in wardrobes, best use of the interior space can be made by creating tailor-made hanging and shelving sections. Clothes organizers of this kind can be professionally made to measure, but in fact they can be constructed from the simplest of materials, at a great saving in cost. A wardrobe up to 2400mm (8ft) wide can be "organized" with just four standard lengths of veneered or plastic-coated chipboard (particle board), a length of clothes pole and some 75 x 25mm (3 x 1in) wood to act as shelf supports.

Start by marking and cutting out the components. All are 300mm (12in) wide. There are two uprights 1930mm (6 ft 4in) long, two shelves long enough to span the wardrobe or alcove, and six small shelves 300mm (12in) square. Sand all the cut edges.

Next, cut two sets of shelf supports to fit the back and side walls of the wardrobe or alcove. Nail or screw the first supports in place so that their top edges are 2140mm (7ft) above the floor. Add the second set 1930mm (6ft 4in) above the floor. Then make up the central shelf unit, using the two uprights and the six small shelves, spacing these to suit the storage requirements. Notch the top rear corners of the unit so that they will fit around the lower shelf support, and stand it in place. Add the lower shelf first, then the upper one, and complete the unit by adding upper (and, if desired, lower) hanging rails at each side of the central unit.

1 Fix the upper set of shelf supports to the sides and back of the wardrobe or alcove, with their top edges 2140mm (7ft) above floor level.

4 Mark the height of the uprights and the length of the shelves required on the components. Square cutting lines across them, using a try square.

7 Stand the unit against the back of the wardrobe or alcove. Mark the position of the lower shelf support on the uprights. Cut notches to fit around the support.

2 Add the lower set of shelf supports with their top edges 1930mm (6ft 4in) above floor level. Check that they are all horizontal.

3 Next, cut the components to width, using a circular saw with a fence or a guide strip clamped across it to keep the cuts straight.

5 Cut the shelves and uprights to the lengths required with the circular saw. Then cut the six small squares for the central shelf unit.

6 Make the central shelf unit by gluing and nailing or screwing the shelves between the uprights. Space the shelves as required.

8 Reposition the central shelf unit, then lay the lower shelf on its supports. Drill pilot holes, then nail or screw down through it into the supports and the shelf unit.

9 Fit hangers to support the clothes rail beneath the lower shelf. Add a second lower rail if wished. Complete the unit by fixing the top shelf to its supports.

STORAGE
PROJECTS

Although storage units are functional, they can often be attractive too. On the following pages you will find three simple storage projects that are just that. A magazine rack is a must for any home, providing a place for newspapers and magazines that have yet to be read. The rack shown has a large capacity, but can be folded up and stored when not needed. A small double-shelf wall unit will have many uses around the home, for books, ornaments and the like. It is made from board and trimmed with decorative moulding. Finally, there is an unusual sloping CD rack, which can be made from wood left over from other projects.

MAGAZINE RACK

This folding rack takes little time to construct and uses a few basic techniques. There are no joints to make, and no expensive tools are required; all you need are the basics of accurate marking out, cutting and fitting together. The interlocking design allows the rack to be opened up or folded flat and stowed away, with no need for clips or catches.

The rack consists of two separate assemblies that form the sides. One slides inside the other and is attached with the two bolts that form the pivot mechanism. It can be made to any convenient size, but if you follow the diagrams, you will not have to calculate the dimensions and angles required for

Materials

- 2.7m (9ft) of 50 x 25mm (2 x 1in) planed softwood for the legs
- 4.2m (14ft) of 75 x 12mm (3 x ½in) planed (dressed) softwood for the slats
- 6mm (¼in) MDF (medium-density fiberboard) for the template
- 16 25mm (1in) brass wood screws
- 2 50mm (2in) brass wood screws
- Panel pin (brad)
- 2 65mm (2½in) coachbolts (carriage bolts), nuts and washers
- Thin cord

the legs. Draw it out full size on plywood or MDF (medium-density fiberboard) to create a template for marking out.

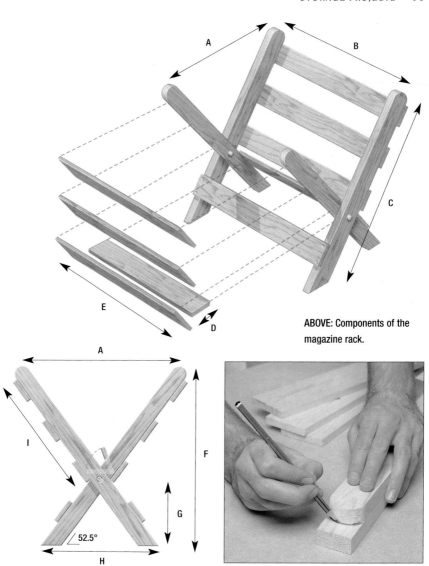

ABOVE: Components of the magazine rack.

ABOVE: End profile.

52.5°

KEY

A	510mm (20in)
B	490mm (19¼in)
C	660mm (26in)
D	75mm (3in)
E	435mm (17⅛in)
F	520mm (20½in)
G	190mm (7½in)
H	345mm (13½in)
I	400mm (16in)

1 Cut the legs and the slats to their overall length. The slats for the inner frame are 55mm (2⅛in) shorter than those used for the outer frame, allowing them to slide easily within the latter. Cut a rounded profile at the top of each leg if wished, using the first as a pattern for the others so that they will be uniform. ▶

2 Lay each pair of legs in turn over the template drawn on a sheet of MDF (medium-density fiberboard) and mark the positions of the slats and pivot point. Support the upper leg with an offcut (scrap) of wood to keep it level. Drill a pilot hole through the pivot point of each leg at this stage.

3 Assemble the inner frame. Insert one screw at each end of the top slat, then use a try square to adjust the assembly before you proceed. It is essential that the frames are absolutely square. Make sure the ends of the slats do not protrude over the sides of the frame.

6 Use two small offcuts of 12mm (½in) thick wood at each side to support the outer legs at the correct level. Screw the top and third slats in place on the outer legs, checking that they are square as before. All four legs of the rack should be parallel with each other to allow the assembly to open and close freely without any binding. If necessary, make adjustments.

7 Turn the assembly over to fit the bottom slat. At this stage, the two frames should enclose each other, but they can still be slid apart if required. Now is a good time to clean up any rough edges with medium-grade abrasive paper, wrapped around a cork sanding block, before proceeding. You could also apply a coat of clear sealer or varnish at this stage.

4 Add the third slat, then turn the frame over to attach the bottom slat. The final assembly will be easier if you omit the second slat at this stage; it can be added when the rack is bolted together. Three slats are sufficient at this stage to keep the assembly square.

5 Use the inner frame as a building jig for the outer frame. Position the components carefully, making sure that the pivot holes are in line. Insert a small panel pin (brad) to keep the legs aligned as you work. Note how the angled ends of the legs face in opposite directions.

8 Drill through the legs for the coachbolts (carriage bolts), using the pilot holes to guide the drill bit. Fit a coachbolt to each side, inserting a large washer between the moving parts to reduce the amount of friction. Fit the nuts on the inside, but do not over-tighten them or you will distort the framework. Note how the bottom slat on the outer frame will act as a stop to hold the rack open.

9 Insert the bottom piece, which acts as a floor for the rack. Cut it to fit between the legs of the inner frame and attach with two long brass screws. It should pivot easily, allowing the rack to be folded flat for storage. Add the remaining two slats. Fix a couple of lengths of thin cord between the bottom slats as a final touch to secure the legs in their open position.

BOOKSHELF

Manufactured boards with veneered faces, sometimes called decorative boards, can make quick work of any project. However, the exposed edges of veneered plywood and MDF (medium-density fiberboard) are vulnerable to damage and not at all attractive. To overcome this drawback, you can buy solid wood trim to match most common types of veneer, or you can make your own if you have the right tools. This bookshelf was made from boards veneered with American white oak, edged with darker oak trim.

The dimensions of this small shelf unit are provided as a guide only. You can alter them to suit your own books

Materials

- 760 x 610mm (30 x 24in) of 12mm (½in) veneered plywood or MDF (medium-density fiberboard)
- 2.7m (9ft) of 19mm (¾in) angled moulding for edge trim
- PVA (white) wood glue
- Panel pins (brads)

or any other items you may wish to display. A suitable height for most paperbacks is 205–255mm (8–10in). Bear in mind that 12mm (½in) boards will sag under heavy loads if you make the shelves too wide. Restrict unsupported widths to 600m (24in).

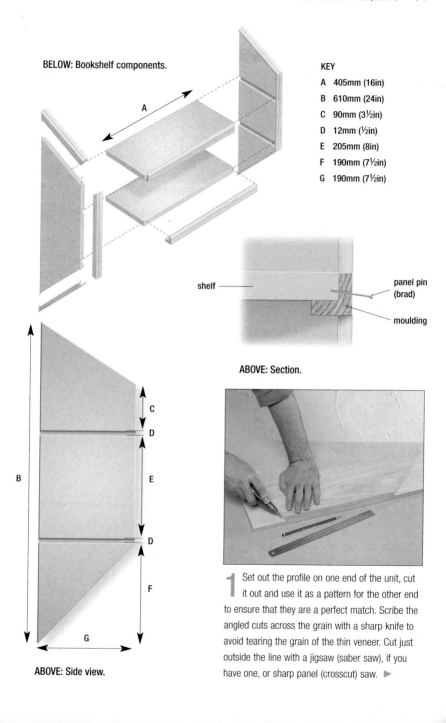

BELOW: Bookshelf components.

KEY

A 405mm (16in)
B 610mm (24in)
C 90mm (3½in)
D 12mm (½in)
E 205mm (8in)
F 190mm (7½in)
G 190mm (7½in)

A

shelf

panel pin (brad)

moulding

ABOVE: Section.

B

C
D
E
D
F
G

ABOVE: Side view.

1 Set out the profile on one end of the unit, cut it out and use it as a pattern for the other end to ensure that they are a perfect match. Scribe the angled cuts across the grain with a sharp knife to avoid tearing the grain of the thin veneer. Cut just outside the line with a jigsaw (saber saw), if you have one, or sharp panel (crosscut) saw. ▶

2 Clamp the angled ends in a vice so that they are horizontal, then plane them down to the scribed lines with a block plane. Work with the grain angled away from you to avoid damaging the veneer. The block plane, with a finely set, sharp blade, is the ideal tool for working this material.

3 Form the housings for the shelves with a router, running it along a straightedge pinned (tacked) to the inner face. To ensure accuracy, clamp the two ends together and cut the grooves in one operation. Pin a strip of scrap wood to the board edge to prevent breakout at the end of the groove.

6 Sash clamps are ideal for holding the assembly steady while pinning the shelves in place. Small panel pins (brads) are sufficient for a small unit such as this. Check that all corners are square – measuring the diagonals is the easiest way of doing this; they should be equal – and leave overnight for the glue to set. Note the small scraps of wood inserted beneath the clamp heads to protect the veneer.

7 Cut two lengths of decorative angled moulding to trim the front edges of the shelves. The moulding shown has a small shadow line, or "quirk", running along its length. This is designed to help conceal the heads of the panel pins after they have been punched down with a nail punch. When buying mouldings for this purpose, always check that their design provides a means of concealing the fixings.

4 The boards can vary in thickness depending on the type of veneer. It is not always possible to match the size of board exactly to the diameter of the router cutter. If necessary, plane small rebates (rabbets) on the underside of each shelf until it fits the grooves perfectly.

5 Apply glue to the housings and slot the unit together. It is good practice to use the glue sparingly. Any excess will have to be removed completely to prevent discoloration of the veneer at the finishing stage. Wipe off with a slightly damp cloth, and avoid rubbing glue into the grain.

8 The same moulding is used to trim the end panels. Mitre the ends at the corners with a tenon saw or adjustable mitre saw. To determine the angle for the mitred corners, place a short section of moulding in position and use it to mark pencil lines on the end panel, parallel to the front edges. Draw a line from the corner to the point of intersection to bisect the angle exactly. Use this as a guide for setting an adjustable bevel gauge.

9 Apply PVA (white) wood glue to the front edges of the end panels and pin (tack) the mouldings in place. Notice how the minimum of glue has been used. This is to prevent any excess from being squeezed on to the veneer surface when the pins are punched in with the nail punch. When the glue has dried, apply coloured stopping to each pinhole before sanding smooth all over, ready for finishing.

CD RACK

The idea for this compact disc storage system came about because a piece of cherry wood, with distinctive figure in the grain, and a short offcut (scrap) of waney-edged yew with an interesting shape was left over in the workshop. You can use any type of wood, of course, possibly something left over from another job. With a little imagination, you can turn short lengths of wood into all manner of items.

The design is simplicity itself – it uses the cantilever principle to support the weight of the CDs. A width of 255mm (10in) will allow two columns to be stacked side by side. The rack can be any height you like, provided the base is wide enough to make it stable.

Materials

- 760mm (30in) of 125 x 25mm (5 x 1in) hardwood for the rack
- 760mm (30in) of 25 x 12mm (1 x ½in) hardwood for the sides
- 280mm (11in) of 150 x 19mm (6 x ¾in) hardwood for the base
- PVA (white) wood glue
- Brass panel pins (brads)

As a guide, ensure that the top of the rack, inclined at 10 degrees, is vertically above the back edge of the base. The diagram shows how to set out the ingenious dovetailed housing joint that holds the unit together.

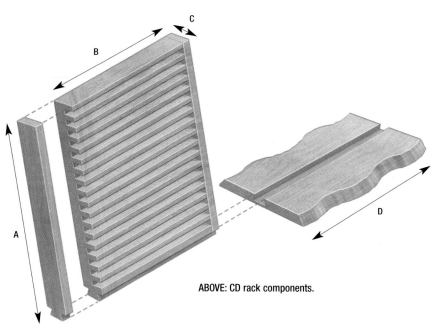

ABOVE: CD rack components.

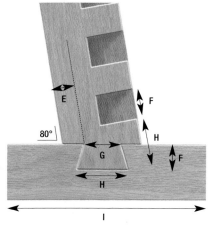

ABOVE: Section.

KEY

A	370mm (14½in)	E	6mm (¼in)
B	255mm (10in)	F	9mm (⅜in)
C	25mm (1in)	G	12mm (½in)
D	280mm (11in)	H	19mm (¾in)
		I	150mm (6in)

80°

1 Cut the 125 x 25mm (5 x 1in) hardwood into two pieces 370mm (14½in) long for the main portion of the rack. Plane the edges square, glue and clamp them together. Simple butt joints are sufficient in this case. To make sure that the board remains absolutely flat, clamp a stout batten over the top of the assembly before finally tightening the sash clamps. ▶

2 Use a 9mm (⅜in) router bit to rout a slot 19mm (¾in) up from the bottom edge. Make a routing jig for the other slots by fixing a 9mm (⅜in) strip of hardwood to the router base, 9mm (⅜in) from the cutter's edge.

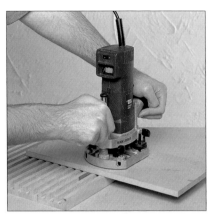

3 It is a simple matter to run the hardwood strip along each slot to position the next groove correctly. Continue in this way to the end of the board. Make sure the work is clamped firmly to the bench when doing this, or use a bench stop.

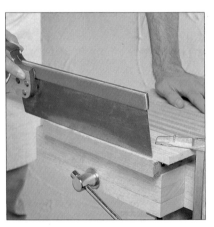

6 Use the same template to mark out the bottom edge of the main upright. Scribe the shoulders along its length with a marking gauge, and clamp a straightedge along the shoulder line to guide the tenon saw. Keep the saw blade perfectly level to ensure the shoulders are straight and parallel.

7 To form the tail on the upright, plane the required angle on a scrap piece of wood to make an accurate guide for a small shoulder plane. Use a paring chisel to remove the waste from the corners. The angles are different on each face because of the sloping profile and should match those on the two side pieces.

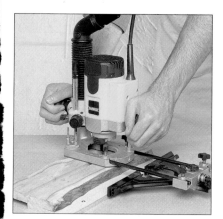

4 Use a dovetail cutter to rout the housing groove in the base. To deal with a waney edge, pin a straight-edged piece of plywood to the underside and run the router fence along it. Screw it down to the work surface so that it cannot move.

5 Cut the tails on the two side pieces with a fine dovetail saw. Use a bevel gauge to set the shoulders at an angle of 10 degrees. Then make a small template to mark the shape of the tails to suit the profile of the dovetail groove.

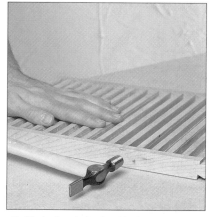

8 Plane the bottom edge of the tail to the required angle to complete the joint, paring it down until the tail achieves a good sliding fit in the housing. Before fitting the side pieces, you should clean up each groove with a small sanding block. Make this from a thin strip of wood and wrap it with abrasive paper.

9 Pin (tack) and glue the side pieces to the upright, using small brass panel pins (brads). Align the dovetails accurately and position the pins so that they avoid the slots. Apply glue to the dovetailed housing in the base and slide the rack into place. Wipe off excess glue with a damp cloth. When the glue is dry, apply the desired finish.

INDEX